Let's find out about...
BEING SAFE

Studio Manager: Sara Greasley
Editor: Belinda Weber
Designer: Trudi Webb
Production Controller: Ed Green
Production Manager: Suzy Kelly

ISBN-13: 978-1-84898-085-3 pbk

Copyright © ticktock Entertainment Ltd 2010
First published in Great Britain in 2010 by ticktock Media Ltd,
The Old Sawmill, 103 Goods Station Road, Tunbridge Wells, Kent, TN1 2DP

Printed in China
9 8 7 6 5 4 3 2 1

Picture credits (t=top; b=bottom; c=centre; l=left; r=right; OFC=outside front cover; OBC=outside back cover):
Altrendo Images/Getty Images: 18tr. Cornstock Images/Getty Images: 16l. Ghislain & Marie David de Lossy: 5bl.
Flying Colours/Getty Images: 18bl. iStock: OFCtr, 5t, 6, 7b, 8, 10b, 23b. JGI/Getty Images: 11tl. Shutterstock: OFCbr,
OFCbl, 1, 4 both, 7t, 9 both, 10t, 11br, 12, 13, 14–15 all, 16r, 17, 19, 20bl, 21 both, 22, 23t, OBC.
Somos Images/Photolibrary.com: 20tr. Hayley Terry: OFCtl and throughout.

Every effort has been made to trace copyright holders, and we apologize in advance for any omissions.
We would be pleased to insert the appropriate acknowledgments in any subsequent edition of this publication.

Contents

How do I stay safe at home?

Home is where we all feel safest. But you would be surprised how many accidents can happen at home.

Danger!

Guns and knives are **dangerous** and can hurt you very badly indeed. If you see a gun or a knife, don't touch it. Tell an adult immediately.

Bottles and pills

Never take any tablets you find, however pretty they look. And never drink anything from a bottle without checking with an adult, just in case it is not what it says on the label.

Medicines should be locked away in a cupboard.

Medicine tablets

Watch out for windows

Never lean out of an open window. It's very easy to fall. Never climb on to or play on windowsills.

Take care when looking out of windows

Playing on stairs

Don't play on the stairs and take extra care when going up or down so you don't fall. Don't leave your toys on the stairs as someone else could trip over them.

Clear toys off the staircase so people don't trip.

Talking Point

Why is it dangerous to climb on furniture?

Furniture looks strong, but it could fall over or break if you climb on it. You might also fall off it and hurt yourself. If you want to climb, do it in the playground. The climbing frames there are designed to be clambered all over!

WORD WIZARD!
adult
Grown-up person

Staying safe in the kitchen

The kitchen is a fun place to be and you might enjoy cooking sometimes too. Make sure you don't hurt yourself in the kitchen by remembering some important rules.

Kitchen know-how

Always take great care around the stove. Make sure an adult is with you if want to cook something and ask the adult to put the cooker on for you.

Always ask an adult to help you carry hot dishes or take things out of the cooker.

Pots and pans

Remember that cooking pots and pans get hot so don't touch them without an oven mitt or cloth. Ask an adult to help you lift hot pots and pans.

Saucepan

Ask how

Always ask before using knives or electrical equipment. Get an adult to show you how. If you want to use a microwave, make sure you know what dishes can be put into it safely.

When you use a sharp knife, keep your fingers away from the blade.

Talking point

Why is it important to wash your hands before cooking or eating?

Always wash your hands before you handle food or eat anything to make sure they are free from **germs** and dirt. If you touch raw food, be sure to wash your hands again before you eat anything. Wash fruit and vegetables before you eat them.

How do I stay safe in the bathroom?

It's good to stay clean and take regular baths or showers. It's important to wash your hands often, too. But hot water can scald you so you need to know how to take care.

Bathtime

Your parents will check the water **temperature** of your bath for you but it's a good idea to learn how to do it for yourself. Dip a finger into the water before you get in to check how hot it is.

Never stand up in the bath. It is easy to slip and fall and you could hurt yourself badly

Think about others

Remember that others will use the bathroom after you. Put the seat down before you flush the toilet and leave it down. This will help stop germs from spreading.

Clean hands

When you are washing your hands, always turn the cold tap on first. That way you won't get burnt by hot water.

Use the cold water first

Talking Point

What are the biggest dangers in the bathroom?

Water splashes can make the floor slippery, so take special care you don't trip and fall. When you are in the bath, never put your head under the water. It's very easy to get trapped or even drown.

WORD WIZARD!
scald
Burn caused by hot water

Fire!

A fire is one of the most dangerous things that can happen in any home. But there is plenty you can do to help prevent fires.

Here's what not to do

Don't play with matches or touch lighters or candles.

Don't put clothes or other things over a lamp or heater.

Don't stand close to an open fire or stove in case your clothes catch fire.

Don't stick things in electric sockets or play with wires.

Fires should always have a guard.

Smoke alarm

What is a smoke alarm?

A **smoke alarm** can tell if there is smoke in the air. It makes a loud beeping noise to warn you so you can get out of the house. Ask your parents if you have smoke alarms in your home.

Talking Point

Why do you need a smoke alarm?

You might not know right away if a fire starts in your home, particularly if it happens at night. The smoke alarm warns you so everyone can get out safely.

And what if there is a fire?

If a fire starts, go outside. Fast. Don't stop to get your toys or go back in for anything. Help your family to make a fire escape plan so you all know what to do if anything happens.

Make a fire escape plan

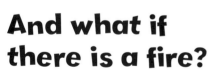

Online safety

Working on the computer is fun and you can learn a lot, but you do have to take care. Ask your parents to help you find ways of using **email** and the internet safely. They can suggest **search engines** and **chat rooms** that are safe to visit.

Don't give anyone your name and never arrange to meet people without telling your parents.

Can I give my name and address online?

Never give out any details about yourself or your family online. Don't tell anyone your name, address or phone number. If you're asked questions like these, tell your parents straight away.

And what if someone asks to meet me?

Tell your parents. If they agree, you could meet the person, but only with your parents and in a place where there are lots of people around.

Tell your parents if something makes you feel bad.

Talking point

Can you chat with friends on the internet?

You can, but check with your parents first. Let them know who you are chatting with. Only chat with people online who you know in real life. That way you'll stay safe.

What if I get a nasty email?

Don't reply. Tell your parents and if it happens again, they might want to get in touch with your email service. If you come across a site that makes you feel uncomfortable, tell your parents. It can happen to anyone and it's not your fault.

How do I cross the road safely?

You probably always go out with an adult, but it is important to know how to cross the road safely.

Crossing the road

Find a safe place to cross. A special crossing with **traffic signals** is best. If there isn't one, find a place where you can see well in both directions. Never stand near a bus or large truck.

Listen

Look both ways

Stop, look, listen

Stop at the kerb, but don't stand too close to the edge. Have a good look both ways to see if anything is coming. Listen carefully, too. Sometimes you can hear traffic coming before you see it. Look again, and when you know it is safe, walk across the road. Keep looking and listening as you walk.

Talking Point

Why is it dangerous to cross the road near parked cars?

The cars make it difficult to see the road properly and drivers may not be able to see you clearly. Never try to step out into the road behind a parked car to try to see what is coming. You might get hurt badly.

Don't run

Don't run across the road. You could fall and then you might not be able to get up in time if a car is coming.

15

Staying safe in cars and on bikes

Always sit in the back seat of a car. It is much safer than the front. Make sure you are strapped in. This means you are secure if the car has to stop suddenly.

Seat belt

Sit up

You'll need to sit on a booster seat until you are a bit bigger. Always wear your **seat belt**. Help your parents by making sure any other children in your car wear their seat belts too.

Always wear a helmet and bright clothing when riding your bike.

WORD WIZARD!
booster seat
An extra car seat for a child to sit in so that the seat belt fits properly

How do I stay safe on a bike?

If you ride a bike, always wear a **helmet**. That way your head is protected if you fall off or have an accident. Wear bright colours so other people can see you easily.

How can I help my parents keep us safe in the car?

Driving is difficult and the driver needs to pay attention to the road all the time. You can help by staying quiet in the car. Never throw things or shout and scream while in the car.

Talking Point

Why do you have to wear a seat belt in the car?

A seat belt is designed to hold you safely in your seat. If the car has to stop suddenly, the belt tightens around you, so that you are not thrown forwards into the front seats or windscreen.

Stay inside

Never try to open the door when the car is moving or lean out of the window. Don't even put your hand out of the window. You never know what might come past.

Stranger danger

To be safe, don't talk to people you don't know. If a stranger tries to talk to you or offers you sweets, stay well away and tell an adult you know as soon as possible.

Never take sweets from strangers.

Don't talk to strangers

If your parents need someone to collect you from school, they will let your teachers know or send someone you know. If a stranger tells you your mum asked him/her to pick you up, walk away fast and tell a teacher. If anyone tries to grab you, yell as loud as you can.

Never go near a stranger's car.

Don't help

If a stranger asks you for help it might seem mean to say no, but don't worry, it is the right thing to do. If they need help finding the way or are looking for a lost dog they should ask another adult.

Why shouldn't you talk to strangers?

Most people are nice, but some people might want to hurt you. If you don't know someone, it's hard to decide if they are being friendly or not. Only stop and talk to people you know. That way, you'll stay safe and won't have any trouble from strangers.

WORD WIZARD!
stranger
A person that you don't know

Staying safe outdoors

It's great to play outside when you can. You might be lucky enough to have a garden of your own or a park nearby where you can go.

Playing in a pool

Water safety

Don't play near water unless an adult is with you. Never go in a swimming pool by yourself.

Safe Sun

If you are playing outside in hot weather, ask your parents to help you put **suncream** on your skin so you don't get **sunburn**. Make sure you wear a hat and some **sunglasses** too.

Poisonous plants

Look at berries, but don't touch

Never eat a plant you find outside. Lots of plants have leaves, **berries** or flowers that are poisonous and can make you ill. Always wash your hands after touching plants.

Playgrounds are a safe place to have fun.

Talking Point

Can you get sunburn on a cloudy day?

Yes! During the hot summer months it's really important to protect your skin from the Sun. If you're playing outdoors, make sure you put on suncream and wear a long-sleeved top and a hat.

WORD WIZARD!
poisonous
Something that can make you feel ill

Being around animals

Cats and dogs and other pets are lots of fun, but need to be treated properly. Even the nicest animal can get cross and may scratch or bite.

Be polite

You wouldn't rush up to another kid you didn't know and start patting him, so don't do this to a dog. Most dogs are fine but some can be scared of strangers and may bite. Always ask the dog's owner first.

Let the dog smell you before you touch it

Never try to touch an animal that is caring for its young or eating. Never tease or shout at an animal.

Wild creatures

Don't go near wild animals, such as snakes, either. Never poke an insect nest. The insects will be very cross and they might sting you.

Wasps' nest

Don't kiss animals or let them touch your face.

Always wash your hands after handling animals.

Glossary

Berries: small, juicy fleshy fruit. Some are poisonous so don't eat any without checking with an adult first

Chat room: an internet site where users can talk to each other using instant messages

Dangerous: something that could do you harm

Email: a message sent from one computer to another

Germ: something that can make you ill

Helmet: a hard hat that protects your head

Search engine: a special program that helps you find things on the internet

Seat belt: belt that is fixed to a car seat

Smoke alarm: a machine that detects smoke in the air and makes a loud noise

Sunburn: a rash on the skin caused by too much sun

Suncream: cream that helps protect your skin from sunburn

Sunglasses: glasses with special tinted lenses that help protect your eyes from the Sun

Tablet: a small pill containing medicine which a doctor gives you when you are ill

Temperature: a measure of how hot or cold something is

Traffic signals: lights that tell the road users when it is safe to drive or walk on the road

Windowsill: the ledge at the base of a window frame

Index